I0409575

Table of contents:

Introduction: The digital Revolution

The "Digital Revolution" in cryptocurrency refers to the profound and transformative changes that digital currencies and blockchain technology are bringing to the world of finance and beyond. Here are some key aspects of this revolution:

1. **Decentralisation**: Traditional financial systems rely on centralised authorities like banks and governments to manage transactions and oversee monetary policy. Cryptocurrencies, on the other hand, operate on decentralised networks of computers using blockchain technology. This eliminates the need for intermediaries and gives individuals greater control over their own financial transactions.

2. **Blockchain Technology**: At the heart of cryptocurrency is the blockchain, a distributed ledger that records all transactions across a network of computers. This ledger is immutable, meaning once a transaction is recorded, it cannot be altered. This technology provides transparency, security, and trust in a trustless environment.

3. **Borderless Transactions**: Cryptocurrencies allow for instantaneous and borderless transactions. This is a significant departure from traditional banking systems, which often involve delays, fees, and restrictions when conducting international transactions.

4. **Financial Inclusion**: Cryptocurrencies have the potential to bring financial services to the unbanked and underbanked populations around the world. Anyone with an internet connection can participate in the cryptocurrency ecosystem, which can be especially beneficial in regions with limited access to traditional banking infrastructure.

5. **Tokenization of Assets**: The technology behind cryptocurrencies has enabled the creation of digital tokens that represent ownership of real-world assets like real estate, art, or even shares in a company. This has the potential to revolutionise the way we buy, sell, and trade assets.

6. **DeFi (Decentralised Finance):** DeFi is a movement within the cryptocurrency space that aims to recreate traditional financial systems (like lending, borrowing, and trading) on blockchain networks, without the need for banks or other intermediaries. This can lead to more efficient, inclusive, and transparent financial services.

7. **NFTs (Non-Fungible Tokens):** NFTs are unique digital assets that represent ownership of a specific item or piece of content, often digital art, collectibles, or virtual real estate. They are built on blockchain technology, providing proof of authenticity and ownership.

8. **Central Bank Digital Currencies (CBDCs):** Many central banks are exploring the creation of their own digital currencies. These would be official, government-backed digital versions of their national currencies, which could potentially streamline transactions and provide additional tools for monetary policy.

9. **Smart Contracts and DApps:** These are self-executing contracts with the terms of the agreement written into code. They automatically execute and enforce the terms when certain conditions are met. This opens up a wide range of possibilities for automating various processes and services.

The digital revolution in cryptocurrency represents a shift towards a more open, inclusive, and efficient financial system. However, it's important to note that this space is still relatively young and evolving. As such, there are challenges, such as regulatory concerns, technological limitations, and the need for continued innovation and development.

2.Chapter 2: Getting Started: Wallets and Exchanges.

Getting started with cryptocurrency involves setting up a wallet to store your digital assets and choosing a platform to buy, sell, and trade cryptocurrencies. Here's a step-by-step guide to help you navigate this process:

Step 1: Choosing a Cryptocurrency Wallet

A cryptocurrency wallet is a digital tool that allows you to securely store, receive, and send cryptocurrencies. There are different types of wallets, each with its own advantages and use cases:

Hardware Wallets: Considered one of the most secure options, a hardware wallet is a physical device that stores your private keys offline. Examples include Ledger Nano S, Ledger Nano X, and Trezor.

Software Wallets (Desktop/Mobile): These are applications or software programs that you can install on your computer or mobile device. Examples include Electrum (desktop) and Trust Wallet (mobile).

Online/Web Wallets: These wallets are accessible through a web browser. They are convenient but considered less secure compared to hardware or software wallets due to potential online vulnerabilities. Examples include Coinbase Wallet and MyEtherWallet.

Paper Wallets: A paper wallet is a physical document containing a public address for receiving Bitcoin and a private key for spending or transferring Bitcoin. They are typically used for long-term storage and are considered highly secure.

Step 2: Setting Up Your Wallet

For Software Wallets (Desktop/Mobile):

Download and Install the Wallet: Visit the official website of the wallet you've chosen and follow their instructions to download and install the application.

Create a New Wallet: Follow the prompts to create a new wallet. This usually involves generating a seed phrase (a series of words that serve as your backup), and setting up a secure password.

Backup Your Wallet: Write down and securely store your seed phrase. This is crucial for recovering your wallet in case you forget your password or your device is lost.

For Hardware Wallets:

Unbox and Set Up: Follow the manufacturer's instructions to unbox and set up your hardware wallet. This usually involves connecting it to your computer via USB.

Generate a Seed Phrase: Your hardware wallet will guide you through the process of generating a seed phrase. Write this down and store it in a secure location.

Step 3: Choosing a Cryptocurrency Exchange

Cryptocurrency exchanges are online platforms that allow you to buy, sell, and trade cryptocurrencies. Here are some popular exchanges:

Coinbase: Known for its user-friendly interface and security features, Coinbase is a popular choice for beginners.

Binance: Offers a wide range of cryptocurrencies and advanced trading features. It's suitable for both beginners and experienced traders.

Kraken: Known for its security measures, Kraken provides a range of cryptocurrencies and trading pairs.

Gemini: Known for its regulatory compliance and user-friendly interface, Gemini is a popular choice for those seeking a secure platform.

Step 4: Registering on the Exchange

Visit the Exchange's Website: Go to the official website of the exchange you've chosen.

Sign Up: Click on the "Sign Up" or "Register" button and follow the prompts to create an account. This typically involves providing your email address, creating a password, and completing any necessary identity verification steps.

Step 5: Verifying Your Identity

Most exchanges require you to complete a Know Your Customer (KYC) process, which involves providing identification documents (such as a driver's licence or passport) to verify your identity.

Step 6: Funding Your Account

Once your account is set up and verified, you can fund it with traditional currency (like USD, EUR, etc.) or other cryptocurrencies.

Step 7: Making Your First Transaction

After funding your account, you can start buying, selling, or trading cryptocurrencies on the exchange.

Remember to exercise caution and follow security best practices when dealing with cryptocurrencies. This includes using strong passwords, enabling two-factor authentication, and being wary of phishing attempts.

Always do your own research before choosing a wallet or exchange, and consider factors such as security features, fees, available cryptocurrencies, and user reviews.

Chapter 3: The Bitcoin Revolution.

The "Bitcoin revolution" in cryptocurrency refers to the profound and transformative impact that the introduction and widespread adoption of Bitcoin has had on the financial and technological landscape. Here are the key elements of the Bitcoin revolution:

1.Decentralisation: Bitcoin operates on a decentralised ledger known as the blockchain. Unlike traditional currencies, which are controlled by central authorities like governments and banks, Bitcoin transactions are verified by a network of nodes (computers) spread around the world, making it resistant to censorship and control.

2.Digital Currency: Bitcoin is a purely digital currency, meaning it exists only in electronic form. It can be sent and received electronically, allowing for borderless and instantaneous transactions.

3.Scarcity and Halving: Bitcoin's supply is capped at 21 million coins, creating a level of scarcity akin to precious metals like gold. Additionally, the "halving" event, which occurs approximately every four years, reduces the rate at which new Bitcoins are created. This scarcity is a key factor in its store of value proposition.

4.Ownership and Control: Bitcoin allows individuals to have direct ownership and control over their funds. Private keys, a form of cryptographic keys, give users the ability to access and manage their Bitcoin holdings without relying on third parties.

5.Security and Transparency: The blockchain, which records all Bitcoin transactions, is highly secure and transparent. Once a transaction is recorded, it cannot be altered or deleted, providing a high level of trust and immutability.

6.Disintermediation: Bitcoin eliminates the need for intermediaries like banks and payment processors in financial transactions. This can lead to reduced fees, faster settlement times, and increased financial inclusivity.

7.Global Accessibility: Bitcoin can be accessed and used by anyone with an internet connection, regardless of geographical location or traditional banking infrastructure. This has the potential to empower individuals in regions with limited access to financial services.

8.Economic Empowerment: Bitcoin provides an alternative to traditional banking systems and fiat currencies. It can serve as a hedge against inflation, and for individuals in economically unstable regions, it can provide a more stable store of value.

9.Innovation and Financial Products: The advent of Bitcoin has spurred innovation in the broader cryptocurrency and blockchain space. This includes the development of decentralised finance (DeFi) applications, non-fungible tokens (NFTs), and various financial products and services built on blockchain technology.

10.Regulatory and Institutional Adoption: Governments and financial institutions around the world are increasingly engaging with Bitcoin. Some countries have implemented regulatory frameworks, and institutional investors are exploring ways to incorporate Bitcoin into their portfolios.

The Bitcoin revolution represents a fundamental shift in how we think about and interact with money and finance. While it has brought about numerous opportunities and benefits, it has also raised important questions about regulatory frameworks, energy consumption, and the broader implications for the global financial system.

Chapter 4: Beyond Bitcoin:Altcoins and Tokens

Beyond Bitcoin, in the realm of cryptocurrencies, lie a diverse array of digital assets known as altcoins and tokens. These are distinct from Bitcoin in various ways, including their underlying technology, purpose, and use cases. Here's an overview of altcoins and tokens:

Altcoins:

1. **Ethereum (ETH):** Often considered the pioneer of altcoins, Ethereum introduced the concept of smart contracts. It allows developers to build decentralised applications (DApps) and execute complex transactions on its blockchain.
2. **Litecoin (LTC):** Created as the "silver to Bitcoin's gold," Litecoin aims to provide faster transaction confirmations and is often used for smaller, everyday transactions.
3. **Ripple (XRP):** Ripple focuses on enabling fast and low-cost international money transfers. It aims to serve as a bridge between different currencies and payment systems.
4. **Bitcoin Cash (BCH)**: A fork of Bitcoin, Bitcoin Cash aims to improve scalability and transaction speed, making it more suitable for everyday transactions.

Tokens:

Tokens are a broader category of digital assets. They are created on existing blockchain platforms, often using standards like Ethereum's ERC-20. Here are different types of tokens:

1. **Utility Tokens**: These are used to access specific features or services within a blockchain platform or DApp. Examples include Basic Attention Token (BAT) used in the Brave browser.
2. **Security Tokens**: Represent ownership of a real-world asset, such as shares in a company or real estate. They are subject to securities regulations and are designed to provide legal ownership.
3. **Governance Tokens**: These tokens enable holders to participate in the decision-making process of a decentralised organisation or protocol. They may be used for voting on proposals or making other governance-related decisions.

4. **Stablecoins**: Designed to have a stable value, stablecoins are typically pegged to a fiat currency like the US Dollar. They provide a way to mitigate the volatility associated with cryptocurrencies.
5. **Non-Fungible Tokens (NFTs):** NFTs represent unique, indivisible assets. They are used for ownership of digital or physical assets like art, collectibles, virtual real estate, and more.
6. **Asset-backed Tokens**: These tokens represent ownership of physical assets like gold, real estate, or commodities, providing a way to digitise and fractionalize ownership.

Chapter 5: Blockchain Technology: The Backbone of Cryptocurrency

Blockchain technology is the underlying framework that powers cryptocurrencies like Bitcoin and many other digital assets. It's a decentralised, distributed ledger system that records all transactions across a network of computers. This ledger is maintained collectively by the network, making it transparent, secure, and resistant to tampering.

Here are the key components and features of blockchain technology:

Decentralisation: Unlike traditional centralised systems, where a single authority (like a bank or government) has control over transactions, a blockchain operates on a decentralised network of computers, known as nodes. Each node has a copy of the entire ledger, and transactions are verified by consensus among these nodes.

Transparency: Every transaction made on a blockchain is recorded in a block. These blocks are linked together in chronological order, forming a chain (hence the name "blockchain"). This chain of blocks is public and can be viewed by anyone, providing a high level of transparency.

Immutability: Once a transaction is recorded in a block and added to the blockchain, it cannot be altered or deleted. This makes the blockchain highly secure and resistant to fraud or manipulation.

Security Through Cryptography: Transactions on a blockchain are secured using cryptographic techniques. Each user has a unique pair of cryptographic keys: a public key (used for receiving funds) and a private key (used for authorising transactions). This ensures that only the rightful owner can access and control their assets.

Consensus Mechanisms: To validate and record transactions, blockchains use consensus mechanisms. The most common one is Proof of Work (PoW), which requires nodes to solve complex mathematical puzzles to add a new block. Other mechanisms like Proof of Stake (PoS) and Delegated Proof of Stake (DPoS) have also emerged, each with its own way of achieving consensus.

Smart Contracts: These are self-executing contracts with predefined rules and conditions. They automatically execute and enforce the terms of an agreement when specific conditions are met. Smart contracts are stored on the blockchain and can be used to automate various processes, from financial transactions to complex operations in decentralised applications (DApps).

Permissioned and Permissionless Blockchains: In a permissionless blockchain (like Bitcoin or Ethereum), anyone can participate in the network, validate transactions, and add blocks. In a permissioned blockchain, access and participation are restricted to a specific group or organisation, which can control who validates transactions and accesses the ledger.

Use Cases Beyond Cryptocurrency: While blockchain's first and most well-known application is in cryptocurrency, its potential extends far beyond that. It's being used in supply chain management, healthcare, voting systems, real estate, and more, as a way to securely and transparently record and verify various types of transactions.

Blockchain technology is a foundational innovation with the potential to revolutionise various industries and how we conduct transactions, moving towards a more secure, transparent, and efficient digital future.

Chapter 6: Investing and Trading Strategies.

Investing and trading in cryptocurrency can be profitable, but it's important to approach it with caution and a well-thought-out strategy. Here are some key strategies to consider:

Investment Strategies:

Long-term Holding (HODLing):

Description: This strategy involves buying and holding onto cryptocurrencies for an extended period, regardless of short-term market fluctuations.

Benefits: It capitalises on the potential long-term growth of cryptocurrencies. It also reduces the impact of short-term volatility.

Considerations: Choose cryptocurrencies with strong fundamentals and use cases. Be prepared for market swings and be patient.

Dollar-Cost Averaging (DCA):

Description: DCA involves investing a fixed amount of money at regular intervals (e.g., monthly) regardless of the price. This strategy aims to reduce the impact of market volatility.

Benefits: It helps smooth out the impact of price fluctuations over time, potentially resulting in a lower average cost per unit.

Considerations: DCA works best with a long-term perspective. It may not be suitable for short-term traders.

Asset Diversification:

Description: Diversification involves spreading your investment across different cryptocurrencies. This can help mitigate risk since different assets may not move in sync.

Benefits: It reduces the impact of poor performance in any single asset. It's a strategy used to balance risk and potential reward.

Considerations: Research and choose assets with strong fundamentals. Be aware that over-diversification can dilute potential gains.

Trading Strategies:

Day Trading:

Description: Day traders aim to profit from short-term price movements within a single day. They make multiple trades in a day, often using technical analysis.

Benefits: It can potentially yield quick profits if executed correctly. It doesn't carry overnight exposure to market risks.

Considerations: Requires a deep understanding of technical analysis, a high level of focus, and constant monitoring of the market. It also involves higher trading fees.

Swing Trading:

Description: Swing traders aim to capture price swings or "swings" in the market. They hold positions for several days or weeks, capitalising on short- to medium-term trends.

Benefits: It allows for more flexibility in trading decisions compared to day trading. It can also be less time-intensive.

Considerations: Requires an understanding of technical and possibly fundamental analysis. Risk management is crucial.

Scalping:

Description: Scalping involves making very quick, small trades to capture minimal price fluctuations. Scalpers aim to make a large number of trades in a short period.

Benefits: Can lead to quick, small profits if executed effectively. It's less risky than other strategies due to short holding periods.

Considerations: Scalping requires a high level of focus, low trading fees, and a reliable and fast trading platform. It may not be suitable for beginners.

Chapter 7: Regulation and Compliance

Regulation and compliance in the cryptocurrency space are crucial aspects to consider, as they help establish legal frameworks, protect consumers, and promote the legitimacy and adoption of digital assets. Here are some key points regarding regulation and compliance in cryptocurrency:

1. Varied Regulatory Approaches:

Global Variances: Different countries have adopted varying approaches to regulating cryptocurrencies. Some have embraced them, while others have imposed strict regulations or outright bans.

Regulatory Clarity: Many jurisdictions are still in the process of formulating comprehensive regulations for cryptocurrencies, leading to uncertainty in the industry.

2. Know Your Customer (KYC) and Anti-Money Laundering (AML):

KYC Requirements: Many cryptocurrency exchanges and platforms implement KYC procedures, which require users to verify their identities. This helps prevent illicit activities and ensures compliance with AML regulations.

AML Compliance: Compliance with AML regulations is essential to prevent money laundering and terrorist financing. Exchanges and financial institutions are often required to implement AML measures, such as customer due diligence and reporting suspicious activities.

3. Securities Regulations:

Token Classification: Regulators determine whether certain tokens or cryptocurrencies are classified as securities. Securities regulations may apply to Initial Coin Offerings (ICOs) or Security Token Offerings (STOs).

SEC's Howey Test: In the United States, the Howey Test is often used to determine if a token is a security. If a token meets the criteria outlined in the Howey Test, it is considered a security and subject to relevant regulations.

4. Taxation:

Tax Reporting: Cryptocurrency transactions may be subject to capital gains tax, income tax, or other tax liabilities. Tax authorities in different countries have issued guidelines on how to report and pay taxes on cryptocurrency-related activities.

5. Consumer Protection:

Fraud Prevention: Regulators aim to protect consumers from fraudulent schemes and scams in the cryptocurrency space. This may involve enforcing strict licensing requirements for exchanges and requiring transparent business practices.

6. Licensing and Registration:

Regulated Entities: Some countries require cryptocurrency exchanges and other related businesses to obtain licences or register with regulatory authorities to operate legally.

7. Blockchain and Smart Contracts:

Legal Recognition: Some jurisdictions have taken steps to legally recognize blockchain records and smart contracts, providing a legal framework for their use.

8. Data Privacy and Security:

GDPR Compliance: In regions subject to GDPR (General Data Protection Regulation), companies handling personal data related to cryptocurrency transactions must comply with stringent data protection requirements.

9. International Cooperation:

Cross-Border Regulation: Given the global nature of cryptocurrency, international cooperation and coordination among regulators are crucial to address challenges and maintain regulatory consistency.

10. Emerging Regulatory Trends:

DeFi Regulation: Regulators are paying increasing attention to the decentralised finance (DeFi) space, aiming to strike a balance between innovation and regulatory oversight.

Central Bank Digital Currencies (CBDCs): As central banks explore the development of their own digital currencies, regulatory frameworks surrounding CBDCs will play a significant role in their implementation.

Chapter 7: Security and Privacy

Security and privacy are critical considerations in the world of cryptocurrency. Here are some key aspects of security and privacy in cryptocurrency:

Security:

Private Keys: Private keys are the keys to your cryptocurrency holdings. They should be kept secure and never shared with anyone. Loss of a private key can result in irreversible loss of funds.

Wallet Security: Choosing a secure wallet is crucial. Hardware wallets are considered the most secure, followed by software wallets (with strong encryption and security features). Mobile wallets are convenient but may be less secure.

Two-Factor Authentication (2FA): Enabling 2FA adds an extra layer of security by requiring a second form of authentication (like a temporary code from a mobile app) in addition to your password.

Phishing Awareness: Be cautious of phishing attempts. Avoid clicking on suspicious links, and verify website URLs before entering any sensitive information.

Regular Software Updates: Keep your wallet software, apps, and operating systems up to date to ensure you have the latest security patches.

Beware of Malware: Use reputable antivirus software and be cautious when downloading files or clicking on links from untrusted sources.

Network Security: Be cautious when using public Wi-Fi networks, as they can be less secure. Consider using a Virtual Private Network (VPN) for added security.

Multi-Signature Transactions: Some wallets allow for multi-signature transactions, which require multiple private keys to authorise a transaction. This can provide an extra layer of security.

Privacy:

Pseudonymous Transactions: While cryptocurrency transactions are recorded on a public ledger, they are linked to addresses rather than real-world identities. This offers a degree of privacy.

Privacy Coins: Some cryptocurrencies, like Monero, Zcash, and Dash, are designed with enhanced privacy features that obscure transaction details, making it harder to trace them.

Avoiding Reuse of Addresses: Using a new address for each transaction can help prevent others from linking your transactions together.

Using CoinMixers or Tumblers: These services combine transactions from multiple users, making it more difficult to trace the origin of funds.

Privacy-Focused Tools: Using privacy-focused browsers, VPNs, and messaging apps can help protect your online activities.

Regulatory Compliance: It's important to be aware of and comply with privacy regulations, such as GDPR (General Data Protection Regulation), especially for businesses and services that handle personal data.

Decentralised Exchanges (DEXs): DEXs may offer increased privacy as they often do not require the same level of identity verification as centralised exchanges.

Educate Yourself: Understanding the privacy features and considerations of different cryptocurrencies can help you make informed decisions about which ones align with your privacy preferences.

Chapter 9: The Future of Cryptocurrency.

The future of cryptocurrency is a subject of much speculation and anticipation. While it's impossible to predict with certainty, we can outline some potential trends and developments based on current trajectories:

1. Mainstream Adoption:

Widespread Use: Cryptocurrency could become a more common form of payment and investment. This may involve integration with existing financial systems and the development of user-friendly applications.

Merchant Acceptance: More businesses may start accepting cryptocurrencies as a form of payment, driven by lower transaction fees and the potential for global reach.

2. Regulation and Institutional Involvement:

Regulatory Frameworks: Governments and regulatory bodies are likely to establish clearer legal frameworks for cryptocurrencies. This can provide more certainty for businesses and investors.

Institutional Adoption: More traditional financial institutions, such as banks and investment firms, may offer cryptocurrency-related services like custody, trading, and investment products.

3. Stablecoins and Central Bank Digital Currencies (CBDCs):

Stablecoins: These are cryptocurrencies pegged to a stable asset, like a fiat currency. They aim to provide the benefits of cryptocurrency without the volatility, potentially making them more attractive for day-to-day transactions.

CBDCs: Central banks around the world are exploring the creation of their own digital currencies. These would be government-backed and could become a new form of digital cash.

4. Increased Privacy and Security Features:

Enhanced Privacy Coins: Continued development of privacy-focused cryptocurrencies like Monero, Zcash, and others may provide more robust privacy options for users.

Advanced Security Measures: Ongoing efforts to improve security in areas like wallet management, transaction validation, and network consensus algorithms.

5. Decentralised Finance (DeFi):

Growth of DeFi Applications: Decentralised finance platforms are likely to expand, offering a wider range of financial services, including lending, borrowing, trading, and more.

Regulatory Challenges: DeFi will likely face regulatory scrutiny as it challenges traditional financial systems and may need to adapt to comply with existing laws.

6. Interoperability and Cross-Blockchain Solutions:

Seamless Transactions: Projects working on interoperability aim to allow different blockchains to communicate and transact with each other. This could reduce friction between various blockchain networks.

7. Environmental Considerations:

Sustainable Solutions: With concerns about the energy consumption of some blockchain networks, there may be a push towards more energy-efficient consensus mechanisms and sustainable practices.

8. Technological Advancements:

Scalability Solutions: Continued efforts to improve scalability will be crucial for handling a larger volume of transactions efficiently.

Layer 2 Solutions: Technologies like Lightning Network (for Bitcoin) and other Layer 2 solutions aim to facilitate faster and cheaper transactions.

9. Education and Awareness:

Increased Understanding: As cryptocurrency becomes more integrated into everyday life, there will be a growing need for education and awareness campaigns to help users understand how to use and secure their assets.

10. Geopolitical Impact:

Currency Competition: Cryptocurrencies may play a role in geopolitical relationships, potentially offering alternative means of conducting international trade.

Chapter : Risks and Challenges.

Investing and participating in the cryptocurrency space presents various risks and challenges. Here are some of the most significant ones to be aware of:

1. Market Volatility:

Price Fluctuations: Cryptocurrency prices are known for their high volatility. Prices can experience significant swings over short periods, which can lead to substantial gains or losses for investors.

2. Regulatory Uncertainty:

Changing Legal Landscape: The regulatory environment for cryptocurrencies varies greatly from one jurisdiction to another. New regulations or changes in existing laws can impact the use and trading of cryptocurrencies.

3. Security Concerns:

Hacking and Cyber Attacks: Cryptocurrency exchanges, wallets, and even blockchain networks can be vulnerable to hacking and cyberattacks. If not stored and secured properly, funds can be stolen.

Phishing Scams: Users may be targeted by fraudulent schemes, where they are tricked into revealing their private keys or sending funds to a malicious address.

4. Lack of Consumer Protections:

Irreversible Transactions: Once a cryptocurrency transaction is confirmed, it cannot be reversed. This can lead to significant financial loss if a mistake is made.

5. Fraud and Scams:

ICO and Token Sales Scams: Some Initial Coin Offerings (ICOs) and token sales have been fraudulent, leading to investors losing their funds.

Ponzi Schemes: Fraudulent investment schemes that promise high returns often target cryptocurrency users.

6. Lack of Regulation and Oversight:

Market Manipulation: The relatively unregulated nature of the cryptocurrency market can make it susceptible to market manipulation by large players.

7. Operational Risks:

Software Bugs and Vulnerabilities: Even well-established cryptocurrencies can have software vulnerabilities that can be exploited.

Forks and Network Upgrades: Changes in the underlying technology or governance of a cryptocurrency network can lead to contentious splits (forks) in the community.

8. Technological Risks:

Quantum Computing Threat: While still in theoretical stages, the advent of powerful quantum computers could potentially break the cryptographic algorithms that secure cryptocurrencies.

51% Attacks: Some smaller cryptocurrencies can be vulnerable to 51% attacks, where a single entity gains control of the majority of the network's computational power.

9. Lack of Regulation and Oversight:

Market Manipulation: The relatively unregulated nature of the cryptocurrency market can make it susceptible to market manipulation by large players.

10. Environmental Concerns:

Energy Consumption: Some proof-of-work cryptocurrencies, like Bitcoin, require significant amounts of energy for mining. This has raised environmental concerns.

11. User Error and Mistakes:

Loss of Private Keys: Forgetting or losing access to private keys can result in permanent loss of funds.

Sending to Wrong Address: If a user sends cryptocurrency to the wrong address, it cannot be recovered.

12. Lack of Scalability and User-Friendliness:

Network Congestion: Some popular cryptocurrencies face scalability challenges, resulting in slow transaction processing times during periods of high demand.

Complexity for New Users: The technical aspects of using and storing cryptocurrencies can be intimidating for newcomers.

13. Geopolitical and Economic Factors:

Government Interventions: Actions taken by governments, such as bans or strict regulations, can have a significant impact on the cryptocurrency market.

14. Legal and Tax Implications:

Tax Obligations: Tax laws surrounding cryptocurrency can be complex and vary by jurisdiction. Failure to comply with tax requirements can lead to legal consequences.